BIBLE
Promise
Book®

The
BIBLE
Promise
Book®

500 Scriptures *for* a
Heart-Shaped Life

KAREN MOORE

BARBOUR BOOKS
An Imprint of Barbour Publishing, Inc.

© 2019 by Karen Moore

Editorial assistance by Debbie Cole.

ISBN 978-1-64352-042-1

Published by Barbour Books, an imprint of Barbour Publishing, 1810 Barbour Drive, Uhrichsville, Ohio 44683, www.barbourbooks.com

Our mission is to inspire the world with the life-changing message of the Bible.

Printed in the United States of America.

Contents

Attitude

It's time to energize your spirit and realign your heart so you think more positively and lovingly about every circumstance you encounter.

God offers you His kind and generous Spirit so you can stay healthy in heart and mind. He nourishes your soul and shapes your heart so you become more like Jesus.

Rejoice in your loving and generous Creator who knows you and who willingly shapes your heart to live in abundant joy. Offer Him your praise and thanks as your spirit grows stronger, lavished by His love!

May God grant your heart's desires and help you live a heart-shaped life.

Create in me a pure heart, O God,
and renew a steadfast spirit within me.
PSALM 51:10 NIV

But those who trust in the LORD will find
new strength. They will soar high on wings
like eagles. They will run and not grow
weary. They will walk and not faint.

ISAIAH 40:31 NLT

Treat others just as
you want to be treated.

LUKE 6:31 CEV

Now may the God of patience and
comfort grant you to be like-minded
toward one another, according to
Christ Jesus, that you may with one
mind and one mouth glorify the God
and Father of our Lord Jesus Christ.

ROMANS 15:5–6 NKJV

Be renewed in the
spirit of your mind.
EPHESIANS 4:23 NKJV

Only conduct yourselves in a manner
worthy of the gospel of Christ, so that
whether I come and see you or remain
absent, I will hear of you that you are
standing firm in one spirit, with one mind
striving together for the faith of the gospel.
PHILIPPIANS 1:27 NASB

Have this attitude in yourselves
which was also in Christ Jesus.
PHILIPPIANS 2:5 NASB

Be tenderhearted,
and keep a humble attitude.
1 PETER 3:8 NLT

♡♡♡♡

Therefore, since Christ suffered for us in
the flesh, arm yourselves also with the
same mind, for he who has suffered in the
flesh has ceased from sin, that he no longer
should live the rest of his time in the flesh
for the lusts of men, but for the will of God.
1 PETER 4:1–2 NKJV

♡♡♡♡

"Blessed are the poor in spirit,
for theirs is the kingdom of heaven."
MATTHEW 5:3 NASB

Awe

Do you ever think about how big God is? Do you sit in awe that He is your Redeemer and Creator and He did it all without a committee? He alone brought you into being and set your feet upon the earth. He alone is in control of the entire universe. He alone chose to love you.

Realizing that, you give up your own need to be in control and even stop asking why. You let the divine greatness of God be the master of all things, including you. Let God be even bigger in your life.

He gave you a big heart because He is a big God!

"Who is like You, O LORD, among the gods? Who is like You, glorious in holiness, fearful in praises, doing wonders?"
EXODUS 15:11 NKJV

"You shall not be terrified of them,
for the LORD your God, the great
and awesome God, is among you."

DEUTERONOMY 7:21 NKJV

♡♡♡♡

"For the LORD your God is God of gods
and Lord of lords, the great God, mighty
and awesome, who shows no partiality
nor takes a bribe. . . . He is your praise,
and He is your God, who has done for
you these great and awesome things
which your eyes have seen."

DEUTERONOMY 10:17, 21 NKJV

♡♡♡♡

The heavens declare the glory of God;
the skies proclaim the work of his hands.

PSALM 19:1 NIV

Let all the earth fear the Lord;
let all the inhabitants of the
world stand in awe of Him.
PSALM 33:8 NASB

♡♡♡♡

"Be still, and know that I am God!
I will be honored by every nation.
I will be honored throughout the world."
PSALM 46:10 NLT

♡♡♡♡

Shout praises to the Lord! With all
my heart I will thank the Lord when
his people meet. The Lord has done
many wonderful things! Everyone who
is pleased with God's marvelous deeds
will keep them in mind. Everything the
Lord does is glorious and majestic, and
his power to bring justice will never end.
PSALM 111:1–3 CEV

How great is our Lord! His power
is absolute! His understanding
is beyond comprehension!

<small>Psalm 147:5 nlt</small>

This is what the Lord says—your Redeemer
and Creator: "I am the Lord, who made all
things. I alone stretched out the heavens.
Who was with me when I made the earth?"

<small>Isaiah 44:24 nlt</small>

The Lord shall reign
for ever and ever.

<small>Exodus 15:18 kjv</small>

Belief

Some of us have tiny faith. We'd like to have BIG faith, but we don't seem to get there. Why? Maybe because we don't ask God to help us build our faith. When we believe He can help with little things, we will ask His help with bigger things.

To have more faith we need a change of heart. We need to trust God is there in the dark days and will bring us to the light.

Set your heart and mind on Him, and you may be amazed at how different your day will be. With Him nothing is impossible.

Then Jesus said to the Roman officer,
"Go back home. Because you believed,
it has happened." And the young servant
was healed that same hour.
MATTHEW 8:13 NLT

And Jesus said to him. . . "All things are possible for one who believes." Immediately the father of the child cried out and said, "I believe; help my unbelief!"

MARK 9:23–24 ESV

♡♡♡♡

When he had gone indoors, the blind men came to him, and he asked them, "Do you believe that I am able to do this?" "Yes, Lord," they replied. Then he touched their eyes and said, "According to your faith let it be done to you"; and their sight was restored.

MATTHEW 9:28–30 NIV

♡♡♡♡

Jesus told them, "I tell you the truth, if you had faith even as small as a mustard seed, you could say to this mountain, 'Move from here to there,' and it would move. Nothing would be impossible."

MATTHEW 17:20 NLT

"God so loved the world that He gave His only begotten Son, that whoever believes in Him should not perish but have everlasting life."

JOHN 3:16 NKJV

♡ ♡ ♡ ♡

We live by believing and not by seeing.

2 CORINTHIANS 5:7 NLT

♡ ♡ ♡ ♡

But we ought always to thank God for you, brothers and sisters loved by the Lord, because God chose you as firstfruits to be saved through the sanctifying work of the Spirit and through belief in the truth.

2 THESSALONIANS 2:13 NIV

By grace you have been saved
through faith; and that not of
yourselves, it is the gift of God.

EPHESIANS 2:8 NASB

Without faith it is impossible to please
Him, for he who comes to God must
believe that He is and that He is a
rewarder of those who seek Him.

HEBREWS 11:6 NASB

Faith shows the reality of what we hope for;
it is the evidence of things we cannot see.

HEBREWS 11:1 NLT

Belonging

When babies are born, the adoring mommies, daddies, and grandmas have great fun discussing the tiny infant's beautiful features. He has Mommy's fingers, Daddy's chin or Grandma's reddish hair. That family resemblance is the beginning of establishing the place where this child belongs.

When you were born into God's family, you started to resemble your spiritual family. Perhaps angels said, "She has her Father's eyes, her Creator's gift for joy or her Savior's gift of grace. She has a heart for God."

God never makes you wonder who your Father is, for He testifies within you, establishing Himself in your spirit, to let you know you are His.

"My sheep hear My voice, and I know them and they follow Me; and I give eternal life to them, and they will never perish; and no one will snatch them out of My hand. My Father, who has given them to Me, is greater than all; and no one is able to snatch them out of the Father's hand."

JOHN 10:27–29 NASB

"My prayer is not for the world, but for those you have given me, because they belong to you. All who are mine belong to you, and you have given them to me."

JOHN 17:9–10 NLT

♡♡♡♡

"The eternal God is your refuge, and underneath are the everlasting arms. He will drive out your enemies before you, saying, 'Destroy them!'"

DEUTERONOMY 33:27 NIV

♡♡♡♡

"No man will be able to stand before you all the days of your life. Just as I have been with Moses, I will be with you; I will not fail you or forsake you."

JOSHUA 1:5 NASB

"See, I have engraved you on the palms of my hands; your walls are ever before me."

ISAIAH 49:16 NIV

♡ ♡ ♡ ♡

But we are bound to give thanks alway to God for you, brethren beloved of the Lord, because God hath from the beginning chosen you to salvation through sanctification of the Spirit and belief of the truth: whereunto he called you by our gospel, to the obtaining of the glory of our Lord Jesus Christ.

2 THESSALONIANS 2:13–14 KJV

♡ ♡ ♡ ♡

I am my lover's, and my lover is mine. He browses among the lilies.

SONG OF SOLOMON 6:3 NLT

And the Spirit himself joins with our spirits to say we are God's children.

ROMANS 8:16 NCV

♡♡♡♡

Be to me a rock of habitation to which I may continually come; You have given commandment to save me, for You are my rock and my fortress.

PSALM 71:3 NASB

♡♡♡♡

For God has said, "I will never fail you. I will never abandon you."

HEBREWS 13:5 NLT

Blessing

Wake up and count your blessings! Before your feet touch the floor with the morning sunrise, thank God for a good night's rest and for the warm bed that kept you feeling safe and cozy.

Thank God for watching over you and for giving you the strength, energy, and presence of mind to begin a new day. Seek His will and His presence for each decision you make and each step you take.

This is your day to count it all joy when you see His face in others and when you reflect His grace to those around you. He will sustain you all through the day.

"The LORD bless you and keep you;
the LORD make His face shine
upon you, and be gracious to you;
the LORD lift up His countenance
upon you, and give you peace."
NUMBERS 6:24–26 NKJV

Then the man said, "Let me go, for the dawn is breaking!" But Jacob said, "I will not let you go unless you bless me."

GENESIS 32:26 NLT

♡♡♡♡

If you try to be kind and good,
you will be blessed with life
and goodness and honor.

PROVERBS 21:21 CEV

♡♡♡♡

He redeemed us in order that the blessing given to Abraham might come to the Gentiles through Christ Jesus, so that by faith we might receive the promise of the Spirit.

GALATIANS 3:14 NIV

"God blesses those who work
for peace, for they will be
called the children of God."

MATTHEW 5:9 NLT

♡♡♡♡

"Blessed are those who have been
persecuted for the sake of righteousness,
for theirs is the kingdom of heaven."

MATTHEW 5:10 NASB

♡♡♡♡

They brought young children to him, that
he should touch them. . .and he took
them up in his arms, put his hands
upon them, and blessed them.

MARK 10:13, 16 KJV

May the grace of the Lord Jesus Christ,
and the love of God, and the fellowship
of the Holy Spirit be with you all.

2 CORINTHIANS 13:14 NIV

♡♡♡♡

The blessing of the LORD makes a person
rich, and He adds no sorrow with it.

PROVERBS 10:22 NLT

♡♡♡♡

Don't repay evil for evil. Don't retaliate
with insults when people insult you.
Instead, pay them back with a blessing.
That is what God has called you to do,
and he will grant you his blessing.

1 PETER 3:9 NLT

Compassion

Compassion is a word that gets to the heart of the matter quickly. It is only needed when a situation is out of control. . .too much sorrow, too little money, too much need. We prefer to share our compassionate hearts more than we want to receive other people's compassion. Yet life happens to us all, and one time or another we each need the kindness, compassion, and forgiveness of someone else.

Make it your primary goal to have a soft heart, one that is kinder and more compassionate to each person you meet. God is working with each of us, to give us more tender hearts.

Shout for joy, you heavens; rejoice, you earth; burst into song, you mountains! For the LORD comforts his people and will have compassion on his afflicted ones.

ISAIAH 49:13 NIV

And He said. . . "I will be gracious to whom
I will be gracious, and will show compassion
on whom I will show compassion."
EXODUS 33:19 NASB

♡♡♡♡

I was eyes to the blind, and feet was I
to the lame. I was a father to the poor.
JOB 29:15–16 KJV

♡♡♡♡

Remember, O LORD, Your compassion
and Your lovingkindnesses, for they
have been from of old.
PSALM 25:6 NASB

He will have compassion on the
poor and needy, and the lives
of the needy he will save.

PSALM 72:13 NASB

♡♡♡♡

Just as a father has compassion on his
children, so the LORD has compassion
on those who fear Him.

PSALM 103:13 NASB

♡♡♡♡

But when He saw the multitudes,
He was moved with compassion for
them, because they were weary and
scattered, like sheep having no shepherd.

MATTHEW 9:36 NKJV

Bring water for the thirsty. . .
bring food for the fugitives.

ISAIAH 21:14 NIV

♡♡♡♡

"Then a despised Samaritan
came along, and when he saw the
man, he felt compassion for him."

LUKE 10:33 NLT

♡♡♡♡

Therefore, as God's chosen people,
holy and dearly loved, clothe yourselves
with compassion, kindness, humility,
gentleness and patience.

COLOSSIANS 3:12 NIV

Contentment

Restless hearts are not contented ones. They search everywhere for a way to calm their stretched nerves and quiet their spirits. They look for antidotes in pharmacies or liquor bottles, hoping for relief from whatever ails their hearts and minds. They exercise until their bodies are too tired to think or so they'll have enough stamina to carry the load again tomorrow.

You can have a contented heart in any circumstance and be at peace because your Father in heaven wants you to be at peace. He gave you the gift of His peace through the Holy Spirit. Embrace Him. Go on your way with a truly contented heart today.

My child, don't lose sight of common sense and discernment. Hang on to them, for they will refresh your soul. They are like jewels on a necklace. They keep you safe on your way, and your feet will not stumble. You can go to bed without fear; you will lie down and sleep soundly.

PROVERBS 3:21–24 NLT

Many people say, "Who will show us
better times?" Let your face smile on
us, LORD. You have given me greater
joy than those who have abundant
harvests of grain and new wine.

PSALM 4:6–7 NLT

♡♡♡♡

I would rather be a gatekeeper in the
house of my God than live the good
life in the homes of the wicked. For the
LORD God is our sun and our shield.
He gives us grace and glory.

PSALM 84:10–11 NLT

♡♡♡♡

When anxiety was great within me,
your consolation brought me joy.

PSALM 94:19 NIV

It's better to enjoy what we have than to
always want something else, because that
makes no more sense than chasing the wind.

ECCLESIASTES 6:9 CEV

♡♡♡♡

"Do not take money from anyone by
force, or accuse anyone falsely, and
be content with your wages."

LUKE 3:14 NASB

♡♡♡♡

Therefore I am well content with weaknesses,
with insults, with distresses, with persecutions, with difficulties, for Christ's sake;
for when I am weak, then I am strong.

2 CORINTHIANS 12:10 NASB

I have learned, in whatsoever
state I am, therewith to be content.
PHILIPPIANS 4:11 KJV

Godliness with
contentment is great gain.
1 TIMOTHY 6:6 ESV

Keep your life free from love of money,
and be content with what you have.
HEBREWS 13:5 ESV

Courage

When a crisis hits you, take it to God and ask for His help. Share your heart with Him and sit quietly in His presence. He will come and listen, and He will not try to give you any pat answers.

Be strong, courageous, and certain that He holds you powerfully in His hand. He cares more about you than anything in the world. He will help you. Don't listen to anyone who tries to blame you or God for what has happened in your life. Trust that God knows your situation and is ready to comfort and bless you.

David also said to Solomon his son, "Be strong and courageous, and do the work. Do not be afraid or discouraged, for the LORD God, my God, is with you. He will not fail you or forsake you until all the work for the service of the temple of the LORD is finished."

1 CHRONICLES 28:20 NIV

Be strong and of a good courage, fear
not, nor be afraid of them: for the LORD
thy God, he it is that doth go with thee;
he will not fail thee, nor forsake thee.

DEUTERONOMY 31:6 KJV

♡♡♡♡

"Be strong and courageous. Do not
be afraid; do not be discouraged,
for the LORD your God will be
with you wherever you go."

JOSHUA 1:9 NIV

♡♡♡♡

David said to Saul, "Let no man's heart
fail because of him. Your servant
will go and fight with this Philistine."

1 SAMUEL 17:32 ESV

"But you, be strong and do not lose courage, for there is reward for your work."
2 CHRONICLES 15:7 NASB

♡♡♡♡

Wait patiently for the LORD. Be brave and courageous. Yes, wait patiently for the LORD.
PSALM 27:14 NLT

♡♡♡♡

But Jesus turning and seeing her said, "Daughter, take courage; your faith has made you well." At once the woman was made well.
MATTHEW 9:22 NASB

But Jesus immediately said to them:
"Take courage! It is I. Don't be afraid."
MATTHEW 14:27 NIV

"I have told you all this so that you may have
peace in me. Here on earth you will have
many trials and sorrows. But take heart,
because I have overcome the world."
JOHN 16:33 NLT

"Be strong and courageous!"
2 CHRONICLES 32:7 NLT

Discernment

Most of us spend a lot of time thinking about the past, even beating ourselves up over poor decisions and past sins. Then we worry about the future and wonder if we'll succeed with our dreams. As a result, we forget to live today and let God lovingly shape us one day at a time.

To live for today requires us to line up our hearts with the guidance we receive from the Holy Spirit. The Spirit of Truth can share with us all the Father has in mind. We are worrying about the future when we have a guide right here and now. Let Him lead you!

For to one is given through the Spirit the utterance of wisdom, and to another the utterance of knowledge according to the same Spirit, to another faith by the same Spirit, to another gifts of healing by the one Spirit, to another the working of miracles, to another prophecy, to another the ability to distinguish between spirits, to another various kinds of tongues, to another the interpretation of tongues.

1 CORINTHIANS 12:8–10 ESV

"Give me wisdom and knowledge, that I may lead this people, for who is able to govern this great people of yours?" God said to Solomon, "Since this is your heart's desire and you have not asked for wealth, possessions or honor, nor for the death of your enemies, and since you have not asked for a long life but for wisdom and knowledge to govern my people over whom I have made you king, therefore wisdom and knowledge will be given you. And I will also give you wealth, possessions and honor, such as no king who was before you ever had and none after you will have."

2 CHRONICLES 1:10–12 NIV

Teach me good discernment
and knowledge, for I believe
in Your commandments.

PSALM 119:66 NASB

I am your servant; give me discernment
that I may understand your statutes.
PSALM 119:125 NIV

♡♡♡♡

The wise of heart is called
discerning, and sweetness of
speech increases persuasiveness.
PROVERBS 16:21 ESV

♡♡♡♡

So you will again distinguish between
the righteous and the wicked, between
one who serves God and one who
does not serve Him.
MALACHI 3:18 NASB

♡♡♡♡

"When the Spirit of truth comes, he will
guide you into all truth. He will not speak on
his own but will tell you what he has heard.
He will tell you about the future."
JOHN 16:13 NLT

And this I pray, that your love may abound still more and more in real knowledge and all discernment.

PHILIPPIANS 1:9 NASB

♡♡♡♡

Reflect on what I am saying, for the Lord will give you insight into all this.

2 TIMOTHY 2:7 NIV

♡♡♡♡

Solid food is for the mature, who because of practice have their senses trained to discern good and evil.

HEBREWS 5:14 NASB

Discipline

Discipline of any sort is not easy. During Lent you may try not to eat chocolate, or at the New Year you may make a commitment to exercise or be more consistent about your prayer life.

Divine discipline offers us a new perspective that can renew our hearts and minds. We may even see the value of the trial we just passed through. Divine discipline is given to help reshape us and remold us to become more of what God wants us to be. If we see it in that light, it can do our hearts good.

Discipline yourself today in ways that will strengthen your heart and mind.

"My son, do not despise the chastening of the LORD, nor be discouraged when you are rebuked by Him; for whom the LORD loves He chastens, and scourges every son whom He receives."

HEBREWS 12:5–6 NKJV

"You should know in your heart that as a man chastens his son, so the LORD your God chastens you."

DEUTERONOMY 8:5 NKJV

♡♡♡♡

Blessed is the man whom You instruct, O LORD, and teach out of Your law, that You may give him rest from the days of adversity, until the pit is dug for the wicked.

PSALM 94:12–13 NKJV

♡♡♡♡

No discipline seems pleasant at the time, but painful. Later on, however, it produces a harvest of righteousness and peace for those who have been trained by it.

HEBREWS 12:11 NIV

I used to wander off until you disciplined me; but now I closely follow your word.

PSALM 119:67 NLT

♡♡♡♡

A wise son accepts his father's discipline, but a scoffer does not listen to rebuke.

PROVERBS 13:1 NASB

♡♡♡♡

I discipline my body and bring it into subjection, lest, when I have preached to others, I myself should become disqualified.

1 CORINTHIANS 9:27 NKJV

For God has not given us a spirit of timidity,
but of power and love and discipline.

2 TIMOTHY 1:7 NASB

Listen to counsel and accept discipline,
that you may be wise the rest of your days.

PROVERBS 19:20 NASB

"As many as I love,
I rebuke and chasten."

REVELATION 3:19 NKJV

Emulate

Do you remember when you were little and played a game called "follow the leader"? You got in a line and whatever the first person did, you did too. If he put his foot in the air, you put your foot in the air; if he laughed out loud, you laughed out loud.

For some people you're the only Bible they'll ever read, the only example of Christ they'll ever see. You live a heart-shaped life because you want to be more like Christ. You want to show His love to everyone. The Lord wants you to help others learn of His love, His saving grace, and His forgiveness.

And we desire that each one of you show the same diligence so as to realize the full assurance of hope until the end, so that you will not be sluggish, but imitators of those who through faith and patience inherit the promises.

Hebrews 6:11–12 NASB

He walked in the way of his father
Asa and did not depart from it, doing
right in the sight of the LORD.

2 CHRONICLES 20:32 NASB

♡♡♡♡

Beloved, now we are children of God, and it
has not appeared as yet what we will be. We
know that when He appears, we will be like
Him, because we will see Him just as He is.

1 JOHN 3:2 NASB

♡♡♡♡

Our faces, then, are not covered. We all
show the Lord's glory, and we are being
changed to be like him. This change in us
brings ever greater glory, which comes
from the Lord, who is the Spirit.

2 CORINTHIANS 3:18 NCV

Therefore be imitators of God, as
beloved children; and walk in love,
just as Christ also loved you and gave
Himself up for us, an offering and a
sacrifice to God as a fragrant aroma.

EPHESIANS 5:1–2 NASB

♡♡♡♡

Be an example to all believers in
what you say, in the way you live, in
your love, your faith, and your purity.

1 TIMOTHY 4:12 NLT

♡♡♡♡

Shepherd the flock of God that is
among you, exercising oversight, not
under compulsion, but willingly, as God
would have you; not for shameful gain, but
eagerly; not domineering over those in your
charge, but being examples to the flock.

1 PETER 5:2–3 ESV

Remember your leaders, who spoke the word of God to you. Consider the outcome of their way of life and imitate their faith.

HEBREWS 13:7 NIV

Follow my example, as I follow the example of Christ.

1 CORINTHIANS 11:1 NIV

Dear friend, don't let this bad example influence you. Follow only what is good. Remember that those who do good prove that they are God's children, and those who do evil prove that they do not know God.

3 JOHN 11 NLT

Encouragement

Nothing motivates us more than seeing the underdog win or applauding as Spiderman tosses out his web and rescues some hapless victim. Heroes are important because we need those we can emulate and those who can rescue us when we can't rescue ourselves.

Jesus was a hero to many people in His day. He is still our hero today. He reached out with kindness, healed those in great need and loved the underdog. He motivated people to want to be better and give more of themselves.

You can share the lifeline you draw upon in Jesus and help restore someone to a sense of hope and grace.

Blessed be the God and Father of our Lord Jesus Christ, the Father of mercies and God of all comfort, who comforts us in all our affliction, so that we may be able to comfort those who are in any affliction, with the comfort with which we ourselves are comforted by God.

2 CORINTHIANS 1:3–4 ESV

Then the church throughout Judea, Galilee and Samaria enjoyed a time of peace and was strengthened. Living in the fear of the Lord and encouraged by the Holy Spirit, it increased in numbers.

ACTS 9:31 NIV

♡♡♡♡

Live in peace with each other. We ask you, brothers and sisters, to warn those who do not work. Encourage the people who are afraid. Help those who are weak. Be patient with everyone. Be sure that no one pays back wrong for wrong, but always try to do what is good for each other and for all people.

1 THESSALONIANS 5:13–15 NCV

♡♡♡♡

So encourage each other and give each other strength, just as you are doing now.

1 THESSALONIANS 5:11 NCV

Some people brought to [Jesus] a paralyzed
man on a mat. Seeing their faith, Jesus said
to the paralyzed man, "Be encouraged,
my child! Your sins are forgiven."

MATTHEW 9:2 NLT

♡♡♡♡

When they had read [the apostles' letter],
they rejoiced because of its encouragement.

ACTS 15:31 NASB

♡♡♡♡

If therefore there is any encouragement
in Christ, if there is any consolation of
love, if there is any fellowship of the Spirit,
if any affection and compassion, make
my joy complete by being of the same
mind, maintaining the same love, united
in spirit, intent on one purpose.

PHILIPPIANS 2:1–2 NASB

If your instructions hadn't sustained me with joy, I would have died in my misery.

PSALM 119:92 NLT

♡♡♡♡

I long to see you, that I may impart to you some spiritual gift to strengthen you—that is, that we may be mutually encouraged by each other's faith, both yours and mine.

ROMANS 1:11–12 ESV

♡♡♡♡

And let us consider how we may spur one another on toward love and good deeds.

HEBREWS 10:24 NIV

Excellence

Defining morality in a world without hard and fast rules has become increasingly difficult. We claim to believe in the Ten Commandments yet find reasonable excuses to allow for exceptions. Morality becomes a word we no longer think necessary.

Peter says moral excellence is one way we grow to know God better. Perhaps, as we understand what real love is and have more love for others, we can understand what it means to be a person who lives heart-first, simply because God created us all.

We may not be able to claim moral excellence, but we can claim Jesus Christ as our Savior and the lover of our souls.

But you are a chosen race, a royal priesthood, a holy nation, a people for God's own possession, so that you may proclaim the excellencies of Him who has called you out of darkness into His marvelous light.

1 PETER 2:9 NASB

In view of all this, make every effort to respond to God's promises. Supplement your faith with a generous provision of moral excellence, and moral excellence with knowledge, and knowledge with self-control, and self-control with patient endurance, and patient endurance with godliness, and godliness with brotherly affection, and brotherly affection with love for everyone.

2 PETER 1:5–7 NLT

♡♡♡♡

"Now, my daughter, do not fear. I will do for you whatever you ask, for all my people in the city know that you are a woman of excellence."

RUTH 3:11 NASB

O Lord our Lord, how excellent
is thy name in all the earth!

PSALM 8:9 KJV

♥ ♥ ♥ ♥

Fix your thoughts on what is true, and
honorable, and right, and pure, and lovely,
and admirable. Think about things that are
excellent and worthy of praise.

PHILIPPIANS 4:8 NLT

♥ ♥ ♥ ♥

"Many daughters have done well,
but you excel them all."

PROVERBS 31:29 NKJV

♥ ♥ ♥ ♥

Who is like unto thee, O people saved
by the Lord, the shield of thy help, and
who is the sword of thy excellency!

DEUTERONOMY 33:29 KJV

An excellent wife, who can find?
For her worth is far above jewels.
PROVERBS 31:10 NASB

♡♡♡♡

Praise the LORD in song, for He has
done excellent things; let this be
known throughout the earth.
ISAIAH 12:5 NASB

♡♡♡♡

But earnestly desire the greater gifts.
And I show you a still more excellent way.
1 CORINTHIANS 12:31 NASB

Focus

When your spirit is crushed, you may decide to put on a happy face. But that decision alone does not always change the way you feel inside. Pray about your sorrow. Ask Jesus to carry it for you and then go out for a walk, unburdened.

Open your eyes to the world around you and focus your heart on the needs of others. Talk to a neighbor, reach out to a friend and find a reason to laugh. By the time you return home, the burden you've been feeling will have lifted, your step will be lighter, and your face will shine with true joy.

Seek the LORD and his strength;
seek his presence continually!
1 CHRONICLES 16:11 ESV

Therefore, holy brethren, partakers of
a heavenly calling, consider Jesus, the
Apostle and High Priest of our confession.
HEBREWS 3:1 NASB

♥♥♥♥

Behold, as the eyes of servants look
to the hand of their master, as the eyes
of a maid to the hand of her mistress;
so our eyes look to the LORD our God,
until He is gracious to us.
PSALM 123:2 NASB

♥♥♥♥

On the glorious splendor of Your
majesty and on Your wonderful
works, I will meditate.
PSALM 145:5 NASB

I will meditate on your precepts
and regard Your ways.

PSALM 119:15 NASB

♡♡♡♡

For the mind set on the flesh is death, but
the mind set on the Spirit is life and peace.

ROMANS 8:6 NASB

♡♡♡♡

For momentary, light affliction is producing
for us an eternal weight of glory far beyond
all comparison, while we look not at the
things which are seen, but at the things
which are not seen; for the things which
are seen are temporal, but the things
which are not seen are eternal.

2 CORINTHIANS 4:17–18 NASB

Fixing our eyes on Jesus,
the author and perfecter of faith.

HEBREWS 12:2 NASB

♡♡♡♡

For consider Him who endured
such hostility from sinners against
Himself, lest you become weary
and discouraged in your souls.

HEBREWS 12:3 NKJV

♡♡♡♡

My mouth will speak wisdom; and the
meditation of my heart will be understanding.
I will incline my ear to a proverb.

PSALM 49:3–4 NASB

Forgiveness

Forgiveness is sticky. It's one of those things we're all grateful for when we seek God's forgiveness to us. We appreciate knowing He has unconditional love for us.

It's not so much fun, though, when we have to forgive someone else. It's even less fun when we don't feel we need to ask for forgiveness. Saying I'm sorry can be difficult. Meaning it deep within the heart can be even more challenging.

Love forgives all wrongs. Sometimes love forgives even without apologies. Love puts all wrongs at the cross of Christ and leaves them there.

That's loving and forgiving at its best.

"And forgive us our debts, as we also have forgiven our debtors. . . . For if you forgive others for their transgressions, your heavenly Father will also forgive you. But if you do not forgive others, then your Father will not forgive your transgressions."
MATTHEW 6:12, 14–15 NASB

How blessed is he whose transgression is forgiven, whose sin is covered! . . . I said, "I will confess my transgressions to the LORD"; and You forgave the guilt of my sin.

PSALM 32:1, 5 NASB

♡♡♡♡

How far has the LORD taken our sins from us? Farther than the distance from east to west!

PSALM 103:12 CEV

♡♡♡♡

If you, LORD, kept a record of sins, Lord, who could stand? But with you there is forgiveness, so that we can, with reverence, serve you.

PSALM 130:3–4 NIV

Then Peter came to Jesus and asked, "Lord, how many times shall I forgive my brother or sister who sins against me? Up to seven times?" Jesus answered, "I tell you, not seven times, but seventy-seven times."

MATTHEW 18:21–22 NIV

♡♡♡♡

"Come now, and let us reason together," says the LORD. "Though your sins are as scarlet, they will be as white as snow; though they are red like crimson, they will be like wool."

ISAIAH 1:18 NASB

♡♡♡♡

"I will forgive their iniquity, and their sin I will remember no more."

JEREMIAH 31:34 NKJV

Hatred stirs up trouble,
but love forgives all wrongs.

PROVERBS 10:12 NCV

♡♡♡♡

"Her sins, which are many, are forgiven,
for she loved much. But to whom little
is forgiven, the same loves little."

LUKE 7:47 NKJV

♡♡♡♡

Your sins have been forgiven
you for His name's sake.

1 JOHN 2:12 NASB

♡♡♡♡

"All the prophets testify about him that
everyone who believes in him receives
forgiveness of sins through his name."

ACTS 10:43 NIV

Friendship

Close friends are essential for our well-being. Few of us survive the journey of life well if we have to walk alone in the world. Some friends assist us for a short time, walk part of the way with us and then move on. Others start the journey with us in grade school and stay connected to us forever. Real friends are with us through lessons we learn, memories we create, and opportunities that flourish and cause us to grow.

Friends with great hearts help each other see everything more clearly. God loves you so much and has provided very special people to show you His love each day.

There was an immediate bond between
them, for Jonathan loved David.

1 SAMUEL 18:1 NLT

"You are my friends when you do the things I command you. I'm no longer calling you servants because servants don't understand what their master is thinking and planning. No, I've named you friends because I've let you in on everything I've heard from the Father."

JOHN 15:14–15 MSG

♡♡♡♡

A man that hath friends must shew himself friendly; and there is a friend that sticketh closer than a brother.

PROVERBS 18:24 KJV

♡♡♡♡

A friend loves at all times, and a brother is born for a time of adversity.

PROVERBS 17:17 NIV

Wounds from a friend can be trusted,
but an enemy multiplies kisses.

PROVERBS 27:6 NIV

♡♡♡♡

"For the mountains may move and
the hills disappear, but even then my
faithful love for you will remain. My
covenant of blessing will never
be broken," says the LORD,
who has mercy on you.

ISAIAH 54:10 NLT

♡♡♡♡

"Greater love has no one than this,
that one lay down his life for his friends."

JOHN 15:13 NASB

Make no friendship with an angry man;
and with a furious man thou shalt
not go: lest thou learn his ways,
and get a snare to thy soul.

PROVERBS 22:24–25 KJV

♡ ♡ ♡ ♡

Do you not know that friendship with the
world is hostility toward God? Therefore
whoever wishes to be a friend of the world
makes himself an enemy of God.

JAMES 4:4 NASB

♡ ♡ ♡ ♡

Say to wisdom, "You are my sister," and
call understanding your intimate friend.

PROVERBS 7:4 NASB

Generosity

Giving is wonderful, and we each must define for ourselves what it means to give. We give our time, our money or whatever assets we have to share. We give whatever we want, but the Lord wants us to give because we have the heart to do so.

Be honest with yourself about how, when, and what you give. When your heart speaks to you to do it, do it. When giving increases your burdens, don't do it. Giving is a matter of the heart and capability, and God wants you to be a generous and cheerful giver.

"Please take my gift which has been brought to you, because God has dealt graciously with me and because I have plenty." Thus he urged him and he took it.
GENESIS 33:11 NASB

"For the poor will never cease to be in the land; therefore I command you, saying, 'You shall freely open your hand to your brother, to your needy and poor in your land.'"

DEUTERONOMY 15:11 NASB

♡♡♡♡

All day long he is gracious and lends, and his descendants are a blessing.

PSALM 37:26 NASB

♡♡♡♡

"Give, and it will be given to you. They will pour into your lap a good measure—pressed down, shaken together, and running over. For by your standard of measure it will be measured to you in return."

LUKE 6:38 NASB

"But love your enemies, do good, and lend, hoping for nothing in return; and your reward will be great, and you will be sons of the Most High. For He is kind to the unthankful and evil."

LUKE 6:35 NKJV

♡♡♡♡

We must help the weak and remember the words of the Lord Jesus, how he himself said, "It is more blessed to give than to receive."

ACTS 20:35 ESV

♡♡♡♡

A generous person will prosper; whoever refreshes others will be refreshed.

PROVERBS 11:25 NIV

They are being tested by many troubles, and they are very poor. But they are also filled with abundant joy, which has overflowed in rich generosity.

2 Corinthians 8:2 nlt

You must each decide in your heart how much to give. And don't give reluctantly or in response to pressure. "For God loves a person who gives cheerfully." And God will generously provide all you need.

2 Corinthians 9:7–8 nlt

You should be happy to give the poor what they need, because then the Lord will make you successful in everything you do.

Deuteronomy 15:10 cev

Gentleness

Gentleness and humility let us give each other room to be who we are. Don't we want to know those around us accept us and love us the way we are? Sure, we test their patience and beg their forgiveness; it's part of recognizing God loves us and is working in us. He expects us to be patient with each other and love each other that way too.

As you practice gentleness and humility, someone is sure to test you to see if you mean it. Be gentle—a lot of battles are going on out there. Everyone around you needs an encounter with someone who lives a heart-shaped life.

> You have given me the shield of your salvation; Your gentleness has made me great.
>
> 2 Samuel 22:36 TLB

Let it be the hidden person of the
heart, with the imperishable quality
of a gentle and quiet spirit, which
is precious in the sight of God.

1 Peter 3:4 nasb

♡♡♡♡

The fruit of the Spirit is. . .gentleness.

Galatians 5:22–23 nasb

♡♡♡♡

If a man is overtaken in any trespass,
you who are spiritual restore such a
one in a spirit of gentleness, considering
yourself lest you also be tempted.

Galatians 6:1 nkjv

Therefore I, the prisoner of the Lord,
implore you to walk in a manner worthy
of the calling with which you have been
called, with all humility and gentleness.

EPHESIANS 4:1–2 NASB

Let your gentleness be known
to all men. The Lord is at hand.

PHILIPPIANS 4:5 NKJV

But we proved to be gentle among
you, as a nursing mother tenderly
cares for her own children.

1 THESSALONIANS 2:7 NASB

Remind them to be submissive to rulers and authorities, to be obedient, to be ready for every good work, to speak evil of no one, to avoid quarreling, to be gentle, and to show perfect courtesy toward all people.

TITUS 3:1–2 ESV

Gentle words cause life and health.

PROVERBS 15:4 TLB

A gentle answer turns away wrath,
but a harsh word stirs up anger.

PROVERBS 15:1 NASB

Good Deeds

At every stage, we have opportunities to do good things to benefit others. When we're young, we may think we're excused from doing good deeds because we're kids. As we grow older and have young children, we may think we don't have time to do good. If we're working our way up the ladder, then our jobs control our lives and we feel too busy. When we retire, we're not certain we have the time and energy to do good.

Sometime we may find ourselves in a place of urgent need. We need to remember the help given to us at every stage of our lives, and then reach out to others any way we can.

He saved us, not because of righteous things we had done, but because of his mercy. He saved us through the washing of rebirth and renewal by the Holy Spirit, whom he poured out on us generously through Jesus Christ our Savior.

TITUS 3:5–6 NIV

"Let your light shine before men in such a way that they may see your good works, and glorify your Father who is in heaven."

MATTHEW 5:16 NASB

♡♡♡♡

"Take heed that you do not do your charitable deeds before men, to be seen by them. Otherwise you have no reward from your Father in heaven."

MATTHEW 6:1 NKJV

♡♡♡♡

But Jesus said to them, "I have shown you many good works from the Father. For which of these do you stone me?"

JOHN 10:32 NIV

Our people must learn to do good by
meeting the urgent needs of others;
then they will not be unproductive.

TITUS 3:14 NLT

♡♡♡♡

Remember that the Lord will reward
each one of us for the good we do.

EPHESIANS 6:8 NLT

♡♡♡♡

Whatever you do in word or deed, do all in
the name of the Lord Jesus, giving thanks
through Him to God the Father.

COLOSSIANS 3:17 NASB

Do not be overcome by evil,
but overcome evil with good.

Romans 12:21 nasb

♥♥♥♥

Just as a person's body that does not
have a spirit is dead, so faith that
does nothing is dead!

James 2:26 ncv

♥♥♥♥

Dear children, let's not merely say that
we love each other; let us show the truth
by our actions. Our actions will show
that we belong to the truth, so we will be
confident when we stand before God.

1 John 3:18–19 nlt

Gratitude

Your business today is to think about all the good things God has given you. Write them down and give Him praise for each thing on your list. Thank Him for the joy you receive from these good things. Hold fast to His goodness to you so that you take nothing for granted. Your health, your home, your job, your family. . .thank Him for the amazing good He has done in your life.

Thank Him too that you can come to Him with a heart of joy, knowing you would have nothing without Him and that every good thing comes to you from His hand.

Give God thanks and praise.

> "Therefore I will give thanks to You,
> O Lord, among the nations, and I
> will sing praises to Your name."
> 2 Samuel 22:50 nasb

The LORD is my strength and my shield;
my heart trusts in Him, and I am helped;
therefore my heart exults, and with
my song I shall thank Him.

PSALM 28:7 NASB

♡♡♡♡

Enter into his gates with thanksgiving,
and into his courts with praise: be
thankful unto him, and bless his name.

PSALM 100:4 KJV

♡♡♡♡

Search for the LORD and for his strength;
continually seek him. Remember the
wonders he has performed.

PSALM 105:4–5 NLT

Be thankful in all circumstances,
for this is God's will for you who
belong to Christ Jesus.

1 Thessalonians 5:18 NLT

♥♥♥♥

For every creature of God is good, and
nothing is to be refused if it is received
with thanksgiving; for it is sanctified
by the word of God and prayer.

1 Timothy 4:4–5 NKJV

♥♥♥♥

Therefore, since we receive a kingdom
which cannot be shaken, let us show
gratitude, by which we may offer to God an
acceptable service with reverence and awe.

Hebrews 12:28 NASB

Every good and every perfect gift
comes down from the Father who
created all the lights in the heavens.
JAMES 1:17 CEV

Thank God for this gift
too wonderful for words!
2 CORINTHIANS 9:15 NLT

A longing fulfilled is sweet to the soul.
PROVERBS 13:19 NIV

Growth

God wants you to grow in love for others. He wants you to grow in praise, admiration, and worship of Him. He wants your heart to grow so big it can hardly be contained in your body. He considers everything you do.

As you seek His guidance today, ask Him to help you develop a greater heart for those things you've overlooked before. Be kinder; be wiser; be conscious of all you say and do. Let your heart lead you into all joy and bring you possibilities only God can give you as you walk with Him today.

But good people will grow like palm trees; they will be tall like the cedars of Lebanon. Like trees planted in the Temple of the LORD, they will grow strong in the courtyards of our God. When they are old, they will still produce fruit; they will be healthy and fresh.

PSALM 92:12–14 NCV

"And why are you worried about clothing? Observe how the lilies of the field grow; they do not toil nor do they spin, yet I say to you that not even Solomon in all his glory clothed himself like one of these."

MATTHEW 6:28–29 NASB

♡♡♡♡

And Jesus kept increasing in wisdom and stature, and in favor with God and men.

LUKE 2:52 NASB

♡♡♡♡

"A good tree can't produce bad fruit, and a bad tree can't produce good fruit. A tree is identified by its fruit. Figs are never gathered from thornbushes, and grapes are not picked from bramble bushes. A good person produces good things from the treasury of a good heart."

LUKE 6:43–45 NLT

I planted, Apollos watered, but God was causing the growth. So then neither the one who plants nor the one who waters is anything, but God who causes the growth.

1 CORINTHIANS 3:6–7 NASB

♡ ♡ ♡ ♡

Rather, you must grow in the grace and knowledge of our Lord and Savior Jesus Christ.

2 PETER 3:18 NLT

♡ ♡ ♡ ♡

We are to grow up in all aspects into Him, who is the head, even Christ, from whom the whole body, being fitted and held together by what every joint supplies, according to the proper working of each individual part, causes the growth of the body for the building up of itself in love.

EPHESIANS 4:15–16 NASB

When I was a child, I talked like a child,
I thought like a child, I reasoned like a
child. When I became a man, I put the
ways of childhood behind me.

1 CORINTHIANS 13:11 NIV

Like newborn babes, long for the
pure milk of the word, so that by it you
may grow in respect to salvation.

1 PETER 2:2 NASB

But the word of God
grew and multiplied.

ACTS 12:24 NKJV

Honesty

We live in a worldwide culture that falls far short of being honest. Honesty appears to be an outdated concept, one that doesn't hold as much weight as it did when Abraham Lincoln walked the earth.

But God wants us to be honest with each other. He wants each of us to seek Him with honest hearts for everything that matters to us.

Thank God for your honest heart. Thank Him for helping you know Him so you can build on a foundation of integrity in every area of your life. Be one more person who is known for being honest.

"God is not a man, that He should lie, nor a son of man, that He should repent; has He said, and will He not do it? Or has He spoken, and will He not make it good?"

NUMBERS 23:19 NASB

The righteous lead blameless lives;
blessed are their children after them.

PROVERBS 20:7 NIV

Truthful lips endure forever, but a
lying tongue is but for a moment.

PROVERBS 12:19 ESV

"These are the things you are to do:
Speak the truth to each other, and
render true and sound judgment in
your courts; do not plot evil against
each other, and do not love to swear
falsely. I hate all this," declares the LORD.

ZECHARIAH 8:16–17 NIV

"The seed in the good soil, these are the ones who have heard the word in an honest and good heart, and hold it fast, and bear fruit with perseverance."

LUKE 8:15 NASB

♡♡♡♡

Listen to my cry for help. Pay attention to my prayer, for it comes from honest lips.

PSALM 17:1 NLT

♡♡♡♡

Therefore, having put away falsehood, let each one of you speak the truth with his neighbor, for we are members one of another.

EPHESIANS 4:25 ESV

I exhort therefore, that, first of all, supplications, prayers, intercessions, and giving of thanks, be made for all men; for kings, and for all that are in authority; that we may lead a quiet and peaceable life in all godliness and honesty.

1 TIMOTHY 2:1–2 KJV

♡♡♡♡

Pray for us: for we trust we have a good conscience, in all things willing to live honestly.

HEBREWS 13:18 KJV

♡♡♡♡

"So my honesty will answer for me later."

GENESIS 30:33 NASB

Hope

Hope gives wings to the soul. It changes the way we perceive the world. When we have hope our spirits are renewed, and we have reason to rejoice. Hope is a matter of the heart; for with hope we see things differently, positively and joyfully.

When affliction comes, though, our patience gets shorter, and we lose hope. Sometimes we even lose our ability or our desire to pray. We wonder if God is still near.

When our hope is down, we can turn our attention to others. We can share with God's people in need and practice hospitality. In so doing, we may discover hope returns.

May the God of hope fill you with
all joy and peace as you trust him,
so that you may overflow with hope
by the power of the Holy Spirit.
ROMANS 15:13 NIV

Be joyful because you have hope. . . .
Share with God's people who need help.

ROMANS 12:12–13 NCV

♡♡♡♡

"So there is hope for you
in the future," says the LORD.

JEREMIAH 31:17 NCV

♡♡♡♡

Jesus looked at them intently and
said, "Humanly speaking, it is impossible.
But with God everything is possible."

MATTHEW 19:26 NLT

My soul, wait in silence for God
only, for my hope is from Him.

PSALM 62:5 NASB

♡ ♡ ♡ ♡

And hope does not put us to shame,
because God's love has been poured
out into our hearts through the Holy
Spirit, who has been given to us.

ROMANS 5:5 NIV

♡ ♡ ♡ ♡

"But now, Lord, what do I
look for? My hope is in you."

PSALM 39:7 NIV

Now faith is confidence in what
we hope for and assurance
about what we do not see.

HEBREWS 11:1 NIV

Looking for the blessed hope and
the appearing of the glory of our
great God and Savior, Christ Jesus.

TITUS 2:13 NASB

"Though He slay me,
I will hope in Him."

JOB 13:15 NASB

Hospitality

When we signed up to be on God's team, we said (albeit in the fine print) that we would be willing to serve however He might need us. That might mean inviting unexpected guests for dinner with a gracious and warm heart or even giving them a place to sleep. It might mean giving to offset the needs of others in crisis.

Each day we need to surrender our plans to the will of our heavenly Father who is the only One who can see the big picture. . .the only One who can see everyone's need.

"When you enter a village, don't shift around from home to home, but stay in one place, eating and drinking without question whatever is set before you. And don't hesitate to accept hospitality, for the workman is worthy of his wages!"
LUKE 10:7 TLB

Be hospitable to one another
without complaint.

1 PETER 4:9 NASB

♡♡♡♡

In that region there was an estate of
the leading citizen of the island, whose
name was Publius, who received us and
entertained us courteously for three days.

ACTS 28:7 NKJV

♡♡♡♡

"Assuredly, I say to you, inasmuch
as you did it to one of the least of
these My brethren, you did it to Me."

MATTHEW 25:40 NKJV

Be. . .hospitable, loving what is good.
TITUS 1:7–8 NASB

♡♡♡♡

At the same time, prepare a guest room
for me, for I am hoping that through your
prayers I will be graciously given to you.
PHILEMON 22 ESV

♡♡♡♡

Keep on loving each other as brothers and
sisters. Don't forget to show hospitality to
strangers, for some who have done this have
entertained angels without realizing it!
HEBREWS 13:1–2 NLT

And after she was baptized, and her household as well, she urged us, saying, "If you have judged me to be faithful to the Lord, come to my house and stay." And she prevailed upon us.

ACTS 16:15 ESV

♡♡♡♡

For I hope to visit you soon and to talk with you face to face. Then our joy will be complete.

2 JOHN 12 NLT

♡♡♡♡

Now the overseer is to be. . .hospitable.

1 TIMOTHY 3:2 NIV

Humility

One of the ways God shapes us is through the gift of humility. With genuine humility we understand that without God we are nothing. Without Him we cannot grow, change, or become all He designed us to be. Without Him we miss opportunities to give and receive love. Without Him we have no real purpose or focus.

With God, though, we discover the meaning of humility. We discover the joy of serving others, of giving more than we ever imagined we could give, of sharing life in every way with those around us. Humility is a matter of the heart.

"But the tax collector, standing some distance away, was even unwilling to lift up his eyes to heaven, but was beating his breast, saying, 'God, be merciful to me, the sinner!' I tell you, this man went to his house justified rather than the other; for everyone who exalts himself will be humbled, but he who humbles himself will be exalted."

LUKE 18:13–14 NASB

My soul shall make her boast in the LORD:
the humble shall hear thereof, and be glad.

PSALM 34:2 KJV

♡ ♡ ♡ ♡

LORD, my heart is not proud; my eyes are
not haughty. I don't concern myself with
matters too great or too awesome for me to
grasp. Instead, I have calmed and quieted
myself, like a weaned child who no longer
cries for its mother's milk. Yes, like a
weaned child is my soul within me.

PSALM 131:1–2 NLT

♡ ♡ ♡ ♡

Pride leads to disgrace,
but with humility comes wisdom.

PROVERBS 11:2 NLT

Better to be lowly in spirit along
with the oppressed than to
share plunder with the proud.

PROVERBS 16:19 NIV

Don't brag about tomorrow!
Each day brings its own surprises.

PROVERBS 27:1 CEV

Although He existed in the form of God,
[Jesus] did not regard equality with God a
thing to be grasped, but emptied Himself,
taking the form of a bond-servant, *and*
being made in the likeness of men. Being
found in appearance as a man, He humbled
Himself by becoming obedient to the point
of death, even death on a cross.

PHILIPPIANS 2:6–8 NASB

"I tell you the truth, anyone who doesn't receive the Kingdom of God like a child will never enter it."

MARK 10:15 NLT

♡♡♡♡

Don't be selfish; don't live to make a good impression on others. Be humble, thinking of others as better than yourself.

PHILIPPIANS 2:3 TLB

♡♡♡♡

Clothe yourselves with humility toward one another, for God is opposed to the proud, but gives grace to the humble. Therefore humble yourselves under the mighty hand of God, that He may exalt you at the proper time.

1 PETER 5:5–6 NASB

Joy

Imagine what it would be like if you decided to rise every morning, maybe even this morning, rejoicing in the Lord. Picture it! You're singing for joy and living in peace. You know, without a doubt, that you are protected, loved, and meant to live fully and well. You're not going to let a negative thought anywhere near you because this is your day for joy. You have the wings of an angel gently wrapped around your shoulders and you know God watches over you and protects you. It's an astounding day!

You will live in joy. You will think joy. Sing joy!

For seven days celebrate the festival to the LORD your God at the place the LORD will choose. For the LORD your God will bless you in all your harvest and in all the work of your hands, and your joy will be complete.

DEUTERONOMY 16:15 NIV

"Do not sorrow, for the joy
of the Lord is your strength."
NEHEMIAH 8:10 NKJV

But let everyone who trusts you be
happy; let them sing glad songs forever.
Protect those who love you and who
are happy because of you.
PSALM 5:11 NCV

But I trust in your unfailing love;
my heart rejoices in your salvation.
PSALM 13:5 NIV

You will show me the way of life, granting
me the joy of your presence and the
pleasures of living with you forever.

PSALM 16:11 NLT

Weeping may endure for a night,
but joy comes in the morning.

PSALM 30:5 NKJV

This is the day which the LORD has made;
let us rejoice and be glad in it.

PSALM 118:24 NASB

A happy heart makes the face cheerful,
but heartache crushes the spirit.
PROVERBS 15:13 NIV

A cheerful look brings joy to the heart;
good news makes for good health.
PROVERBS 15:30 NLT

Always be joyful.
1 THESSALONIANS 5:16 NLT

Kindness

What are the gifts of kindness? Is it when you buy a gift for someone's birthday? When you make a meal for someone in your church family who suffers from illness? Is it when you thank God for His incredible kindness to you? It is all those things and much more.

Remind yourself how blessed you are to live under the kindness of God's grace and how happy it makes you to look forward to the future. Make it a mission within your heart to share that kindness with as many people as you can.

Let your heart be shaped with kindness and a generous spirit.

But the LORD was with Joseph and
showed him kindness and caused
the prison warden to like Joseph.
GENESIS 39:21 NCV

"In Your lovingkindness You have led the people whom You have redeemed; in Your strength You have guided them to Your holy habitation."

EXODUS 15:13 NASB

♡♡♡♡

Because thy lovingkindness is better than life, my lips shall praise thee.

PSALM 63:3 KJV

♡♡♡♡

Don't ever forget kindness and truth. Wear them like a necklace. Write them on your heart as if on a tablet. Then you will be respected and will please both God and people.

PROVERBS 3:3–4 NCV

You will be well rewarded for saying something kind, but all some people think about is how to be cruel and mean.

PROVERBS 13:2 CEV

♡♡♡♡

She opens her mouth in wisdom, and the teaching of kindness is on her tongue.

PROVERBS 31:26 NASB

♡♡♡♡

Christ has also introduced us to God's undeserved kindness on which we take our stand. So we are happy, as we look forward to sharing in the glory of God.

ROMANS 5:2 CEV

Be kind to one another, tender-hearted,
forgiving each other, just as God in
Christ also has forgiven you.
EPHESIANS 4:32 NASB

And the Lord's servant must not be
quarrelsome but must be kind to
everyone, able to teach, not resentful.
2 TIMOTHY 2:24 NIV

Your own soul is nourished
when you are kind.
PROVERBS 11:17 TLB

Leadership

The call to leadership, whether you're male or female, is not one to take lightly. Whether your role is religious or political, or you're a teacher or the head of your household, your leadership is important to the success of those around you.

Leaders look out for those in their care. A great leader is often a great servant, and a leader with a great heart shepherds his flock. As believers, we have the authority of Jesus who leads us only with His love.

May we be called to the leadership of love wherever we are, so that our hearts are prepared and shaped to serve.

But we request of you, brethren,
that you appreciate those who diligently
labor among you, and have charge over
you in the Lord and give you instruction,
and that you esteem them very highly
in love because of their work.

1 THESSALONIANS 5:12–13 NASB

Then the LORD turned to him and said,
"Go in this might of yours, and you
shall save Israel from the hand of the
Midianites. Have I not sent you?"

JUDGES 6:14 NKJV

♡♡♡♡

Lead me in Your truth and teach me,
for You are the God of my salvation;
for You I wait all the day.

PSALM 25:5 NASB

♡♡♡♡

Then I heard the voice of the Lord saying,
"Whom shall I send? And who will go for
us?" And I said, "Here am I. Send me!"

ISAIAH 6:8 NIV

As they ministered to the Lord and
fasted, the Holy Spirit said, "Now
separate to Me Barnabas and Saul for
the work to which I have called them."

ACTS 13:2 NKJV

♡♡♡♡

Now get up and stand on your feet.
I have appeared to you to appoint you
as a servant and as a witness of what
you have seen and will see of me.

ACTS 26:16 NIV

♡♡♡♡

Having then gifts differing according to
the grace that is given to us, let us use
them. . .he who leads, with diligence.

ROMANS 12:6, 8 NKJV

What I say is true: Anyone wanting to become an overseer desires a good work.

1 Timothy 3:1 ncv

♡♡♡♡

Let the elders who rule well be counted worthy of double honor, especially those who labor in the word and doctrine.

1 Timothy 5:17 nkjv

♡♡♡♡

To this you were called, because Christ suffered for you, leaving you an example, that you should follow in his steps.

1 Peter 2:21 niv

Learning

Sometimes it feels like planet Earth is a school, and we're just here to learn our lessons. Perhaps there's some truth to that because once God gave us breath, He started guiding us and helping us understand what He wanted from us. He has been teaching us our whole lives, and it feels good to know we're getting divine guidance.

Think about all the things you have learned so far. Then ask God what else He would like you to know. What else can you do to grow more generous and loving? Share your heart with God and let Him mold you into the person He knows you can be.

I will bless the LORD who guides me;
even at night my heart instructs me.
I know the LORD is always with me. I will
not be shaken, for he is right beside me.
PSALM 16:7–8 NLT

Now as they observed the confidence
of Peter and John and understood that
they were uneducated and untrained men,
they were amazed, and began to recognize
them as having been with Jesus.

ACTS 4:13 NASB

♡♡♡♡

Teach me Your way, O LORD, and lead me in
a smooth path, because of my enemies.

PSALM 27:11 NKJV

♡♡♡♡

Let the wise listen and add to their learning,
and let the discerning get guidance.

PROVERBS 1:5 NIV

Give instruction to a wise man,
and he will be still wiser; teach a just
man, and he will increase in learning.

Proverbs 9:9 nkjv

♥♥♥♥

They were amazed at His teaching;
for He was teaching them as one having
authority, and not as the scribes.

Mark 1:22 nasb

♥♥♥♥

For everything that was written in the
past was written to teach us, so that
through the endurance taught in the
Scriptures and the encouragement
they provide we might have hope.

Romans 15:4 niv

Study to shew thyself approved
unto God, a workman that
needeth not to be ashamed,
rightly dividing the word of truth.

2 TIMOTHY 2:15 KJV

♡ ♡ ♡ ♡

Though He was a Son, yet He
learned obedience by the
things which He suffered.

HEBREWS 5:8 NKJV

Loving God

God commanded us to love Him, to make Him a priority and to do so with the biggest love we can possibly muster. Right after that, He said to love each other, even as much as we love ourselves. Love is what motivates your heart every morning. . .what makes you see the world through His eyes.

Rejoice in your loving and generous Creator, who knows you and who willingly shapes your heart to live in abundant joy. Offer Him your praise and thanks as your spirit grows stronger, lavished by His love!

We love, because He loved us first. If someone says, "I love God," and hates his brother, he is a liar; for the one who does not love his brother whom he has seen, cannot love God whom he has not seen. And this commandment we have from Him, that the one who loves God should love his brother also.

1 JOHN 4:19–21 NASB

"Understand, therefore, that the LORD your God is indeed God. He is the faithful God who keeps his covenant for a thousand generations and lavishes his unfailing love on those who love him and obey his commands."

DEUTERONOMY 7:9 NLT

♡♡♡♡

"Choose to love the LORD your God and to obey him and to cling to him, for he is your life and the length of your days."

DEUTERONOMY 30:20 TLB

♡♡♡♡

Whom have I in heaven but You? And besides You, I desire nothing on earth.

PSALM 73:25 NASB

Jesus said, "'Love the Lord your God with all your passion and prayer and intelligence.' This is the most important [of God's commands], the first on any list."

MATTHEW 22:37–38 MSG

♥♥♥♥

"You must love the LORD your God with all your heart, all your soul, all your mind, and all your strength."

MARK 12:30 NLT

♥♥♥♥

We know that God causes all things to work together for good to those who love God, to those who are called according to His purpose.

ROMANS 8:28 NASB

"He who has My commandments and keeps them is the one who loves Me."

JOHN 14:21 NASB

❤❤❤❤

If anyone obeys his word, love for God is truly made complete in them. This is how we know we are in him.

1 JOHN 2:5 NIV

❤❤❤❤

In this is love, not that we loved God, but that He loved us and sent His Son to be the propitiation for our sins.

1 JOHN 4:10 NASB

"Lord, teach us to pray."

LUKE 11:1 NKJV

Loving Others

Sometimes you treat others with kindness, and they still throw you under the bus or tell lies about you. It's possible that even your friends will betray you. When those things happen and your heart is broken, it's not easy to do it God's way. But the Scripture answer is pretty clear: "Love, do good, bless and pray."

Abusive actions of others give us no excuses to be abusive in return. Instead, we are given opportunities in difficult moments to put Jesus into action, to show God's love, even if we can't quite show our own.

"So now I am giving you a new commandment: Love each other. Just as I have loved you, you should love each other. Your love for one another will prove to the world that you are my disciples."

JOHN 13:34–35 NLT

Owe no one anything except to love
one another, for he who loves
another has fulfilled the law.

ROMANS 13:8 NKJV

♥ ♥ ♥ ♥

Love suffers long and is kind; love does
not envy; love does not parade itself,
is not puffed up; does not behave rudely,
does not seek its own, is not provoked,
thinks no evil; does not rejoice in iniquity,
but rejoices in the truth; bears all things,
believes all things, hopes all things,
endures all things.

1 CORINTHIANS 13:4–7 NKJV

♥ ♥ ♥ ♥

Walk in love, just as Christ also loved
you and gave Himself up for us.

EPHESIANS 5:2 NASB

Love each other with genuine affection,
and take delight in honoring each other.

ROMANS 12:10 NLT

♡♡♡♡

May the Lord make your love for
each other and for everyone else
grow by leaps and bounds.

1 THESSALONIANS 3:12 CEV

♡♡♡♡

"I've told you these things for a purpose:
that my joy might be your joy, and your
joy wholly mature. This is my command:
Love one another the way I loved you.
This is the very best way to love."

JOHN 15:11–12 MSG

All of you should be of one mind.
Sympathize with each other. Love
each other as brothers and sisters.

1 PETER 3:8 NLT

♡♡♡♡

Most important of all, continue
to show deep love for each other,
for love covers a multitude of sins.

1 PETER 4:8 NLT

♡♡♡♡

Hatred stirs up strife, but love
covers all transgressions.

PROVERBS 10:12 NASB

Loving Ourselves

A command to love others as we love ourselves puts some of us in jeopardy. In part, it's because we've bought into the negative things others have said about us, or we have decided we're not lovable. We don't know how to love ourselves, and we're not good at loving others. In fact, we're not sure what this command means.

God sees you. He loves you, imperfections and all. He doesn't love you for what you aren't. He loves you for who you are!

May you awaken today to the love God pours out from His heart to yours.

For You formed my inward parts;
You wove me in my mother's womb.
I will give thanks to You, for I am
fearfully and wonderfully made.
PSALM 139:13–14 NASB

How precious also are Your thoughts
to me, O God! How great is the sum
of them! If I should count them, they
would be more in number than the sand.

PSALM 139:17–18 NKJV

♡♡♡♡

The LORD appeared to him from afar,
saying, "I have loved you with an
everlasting love; therefore I have
drawn you with lovingkindness."

JEREMIAH 31:3 NASB

♡♡♡♡

Come unto me, all ye that labour and
are heavy laden, and I will give you rest.
Take my yoke upon you, and learn of me;
for I am meek and lowly in heart: and ye
shall find rest unto your souls.

MATTHEW 11:28–29 KJV

Jesus said, "'Love the Lord your God with all your passion and prayer and intelligence.' This is the most important, the first on any list. But there is a second to set alongside it: 'Love others as well as you love yourself.' These two commands are pegs; everything in God's Law and the Prophets hangs from them."

MATTHEW 22:37–40 MSG

"Love others as much
as you love yourself."

MARK 12:31 CEV

For the whole Law is fulfilled in one word, in the statement, "You shall love your neighbor as yourself."

GALATIANS 5:14 NASB

For no man ever yet hated his own flesh;
but nourisheth and cherisheth it,
even as the Lord the church.

EPHESIANS 5:29 KJV

♡♡♡♡

If, however, you are fulfilling the
royal law according to the Scripture,
"You shall love your neighbor as
yourself," you are doing well.

JAMES 2:8 NASB

♡♡♡♡

"Do not seek revenge or bear a grudge
against anyone among your people, but love
your neighbor as yourself. I am the LORD."

LEVITICUS 19:18 NIV

Mercy

What an awesome promise that God's mercies are new and fresh every day. That means you're not relying on yesterday's quota for mercy and hoping with all your might that enough is left for today.

You can pick a new bunch of mercies like grapes from a vine because you are part of the real Vine. You can draw near to Him and allow Him to anoint your day, your family and your work so you can be at peace. You can start again with a clean slate.

This is not a small promise!

Let your heart rejoice as you live today in the abundance of God's grace and mercy!

I will sing of thy power; yea, I will sing aloud of thy mercy in the morning: for thou hast been my defence and refuge in the day of my trouble.

PSALM 59:16 KJV

As the heaven is high above the earth,
so great is his mercy toward them that
fear him. . . . For he knoweth our frame;
he remembereth that we are dust.

PSALM 103:11, 14 KJV

The LORD is good to all, and His
mercies are over all His works.

PSALM 145:9 NASB

In His love and in His mercy He
redeemed them, and He lifted them
and carried them all the days of old.

ISAIAH 63:9 NASB

The faithful love of the LORD never
ends! His mercies never cease.
Great is his faithfulness; his mercies
begin afresh each morning.

LAMENTATIONS 3:22–23 NLT

♡♡♡♡

He has shown you, O man, what is good;
and what does the LORD require of you
but to do justly, to love mercy, and to
walk humbly with your God?

MICAH 6:8 NKJV

♡♡♡♡

He does not retain His anger forever,
because He delights in mercy.

MICAH 7:18 NKJV

"Be merciful, just as your
Father is merciful."
LUKE 6:36 NASB

♡♡♡♡

God, who is rich in mercy, because of
His great love with which He loved us,
even when we were dead in trespasses,
made us alive together with Christ
(by grace you have been saved).
EPHESIANS 2:4–5 NKJV

♡♡♡♡

May God give you more and
more mercy, peace, and love.
JUDE 2 NLT

Neighborliness

*Your challenge today is to see your neighbor.
Get to know someone new. Be intentional
about meeting people you have barely
known and show them what God has done
in your life. Ask them to share the ways God
has shown up in their lives.*

*Find out the name of your mail carrier,
your dry cleaner, or the paper boy. The older
man who walks by your house every day has
a name. The grocer and the guy who picks
up the trash do too.*

*If you get to know those around you, your
heart will grow and no one will be invisible.*

Do not withhold good from those who
deserve it when it's in your power to
help them. If you can help your neighbor
now, don't say, "Come back tomorrow,
and then I'll help you."
PROVERBS 3:27–28 NLT

Do not devise harm against your neighbor,
while he lives securely beside you.

PROVERBS 3:29 NASB

Better is a neighbor who is
near than a brother far away.

PROVERBS 27:10 NASB

If you extend your soul to the hungry and
satisfy the afflicted soul, then your light
shall dawn in the darkness, and your
darkness shall be as the noonday.

ISAIAH 58:10 NKJV

"I was hungry and you fed me, I was thirsty and you gave me a drink, I was homeless and you gave me a room, I was shivering and you gave me clothes, I was sick and you stopped to visit, I was in prison and you came to me."

MATTHEW 25:35–36 MSG

"Do to others as you would
like them to do to you."

LUKE 6:31 NLT

If possible, so far as it depends
on you, be at peace with all men.

ROMANS 12:18 NASB

Love does no wrong to a neighbor;
therefore love is the fulfillment of the law.
ROMANS 13:10 NASB

Don't get tired of helping others. You will
be rewarded when the time is right, if you
don't give up. We should help people
whenever we can, especially if they
are followers of the Lord.
GALATIANS 6:9–10 CEV

How wonderful and pleasant it is when
brothers live together in harmony!
PSALM 133:1 NLT

Patience

Did you ever wait in a long line for something you really wanted? Maybe you were eager to get special theater tickets or you were excited to ride your favorite roller coaster at the amusement park. Or perhaps you found yourself sitting in traffic that wouldn't budge and you think you could have walked home faster.

If we believe God is in the details of our lives, then we can afford to be a little more patient with others and with ourselves. As you stand in the endless lines of life, allow for His perfect timing, pray for inner peace, and be gracious. It will do your heart good.

I wait for the LORD, my soul waits, and in His word I do hope. My soul waits for the Lord more than those who watch for the morning.

PSALM 130:5–6 NKJV

The end of a matter is better than its beginning; patience of spirit is better than haughtiness of spirit.

ECCLESIASTES 7:8 NASB

The fruit of the Spirit is. . .patience.

GALATIANS 5:22 NASB

But for that very reason I was shown mercy so that in me, the worst of sinners, Christ Jesus might display his immense patience as an example for those who would believe in him and receive eternal life.

1 TIMOTHY 1:16 NIV

Be patient with everyone.

1 Thessalonians 5:14 ncv

♡♡♡♡

You have need of endurance, so that
after you have done the will of God,
you may receive the promise.

Hebrews 10:36 nkjv

♡♡♡♡

Consider it all joy, my brethren, when
you encounter various trials, knowing
that the testing of your faith produces
endurance. And let endurance have its
perfect result, so that you may be perfect
and complete, lacking in nothing.

James 1:2–4 nasb

Therefore be patient, brethren, until the coming of the Lord. The farmer waits for the precious produce of the soil, being patient about it, until it gets the early and late rains. You too be patient; strengthen your hearts, for the coming of the Lord is near.

JAMES 5:7–8 NASB

♡♡♡♡

Do not forget this one thing, dear friends: With the Lord a day is like a thousand years, and a thousand years are like a day. The Lord is not slow in keeping his promise, as some understand slowness. Instead he is patient with you.

2 PETER 3:8–9 NIV

♡♡♡♡

Patient people have great understanding, but people with quick tempers show their foolishness.

PROVERBS 14:29 NCV

Peacefulness

If you listen to news programs with any regularity, it doesn't take long to recognize we're a long way from world peace.

It's a pretty good bet that even if the world could give you a sense of peace it would disappear again with the next news broadcast.

So what kind of peace does Jesus give? It's the kind that passes all understanding, the kind that keeps you calm and content no matter what is playing out on the world stage.

Peace comes from knowing the One who walks beside you and guides your steps every day—the kind that allows Jesus to shape your heart.

You will keep him in perfect peace,
whose mind is stayed on You,
because he trusts in You.
ISAIAH 26:3 NKJV

"All who listen to me [Wisdom] will live in peace, untroubled by fear of harm."

PROVERBS 1:33 NLT

♡♡♡♡

The peace of God, which surpasses all comprehension, will guard your hearts and your minds in Christ Jesus.

PHILIPPIANS 4:7 NASB

♡♡♡♡

How beautiful on the mountains are the feet of those who bring good news, who proclaim peace, who bring good tidings, who proclaim salvation, who say to Zion, "Your God reigns!"

ISAIAH 52:7 NIV

God blesses those people who make peace.
They will be called his children!

MATTHEW 5:9 CEV

♥ ♥ ♥ ♥

When I was really hurting, I prayed to the
LORD. He answered my prayer, and took my
worries away. The LORD is on my side, and I
am not afraid of what others can do to me.

PSALM 118:5–6 CEV

♥ ♥ ♥ ♥

"Peace I leave with you; my peace I
give you. I do not give to you as the
world gives. Do not let your hearts
be troubled and do not be afraid."

JOHN 14:27 NIV

Each one of you is part of the body
of Christ, and you were chosen
to live together in peace.
COLOSSIANS 3:15 CEV

Live in peace with each other.
1 THESSALONIANS 5:13 NCV

Search for peace,
and work to maintain it.
PSALM 34:14 NLT

Perseverance

When you ask, when you knock, when you search for God, He answers. Sometimes you may not recognize the answer, but the truth is you are connected to God and He provides for your needs as quickly as possible.

If you're waiting for His answers, keep asking. Ask with all your heart, and you will receive. Believe with everything you've got, and you will receive. Knock louder than you've ever knocked before. Give God time to answer in the best way for you. Sometimes you and He have to work out the answer together.

Give Him a call. He hears your heart already.

Work hard at whatever you do.
ECCLESIASTES 9:10 CEV

"Ask, and you will receive. Search, and you will find. Knock, and the door will be opened for you. Everyone who asks will receive. Everyone who searches will find. And the door will be opened for everyone who knocks."

MATTHEW 7:7–8 CEV

♡♡♡♡

We also glory in our sufferings, because we know that suffering produces perseverance; perseverance, character; and character, hope.

ROMANS 5:3–4 NIV

♡♡♡♡

In all these things we are more than conquerors through Him who loved us.

ROMANS 8:37 NKJV

Whatever you do, work at it with all
your heart, as working for the Lord,
not for human masters.

Colossians 3:23 niv

♡♡♡♡

"He who overcomes, I will grant to him
to sit down with Me on My throne, as I
also overcame and sat down with
My Father on His throne."

Revelation 3:21 nasb

♡♡♡♡

Therefore, among God's churches we boast
about your perseverance and faith in all the
persecutions and trials you are enduring.

2 Thessalonians 1:4 niv

Pursue. . .perseverance.

1 TIMOTHY 6:11 NASB

"To the one who is victorious and does my will to the end, I will give authority over the nations."

REVELATION 2:26 NIV

"If you do not stand firm in your faith, you will not stand at all."

ISAIAH 7:9 NIV

Praise

When you praise the Lord with your heart,
mind, and soul, you are instantly lifted into
the heavenly realms of grace and joy. He
transports your spirit and brings it closer to
Him with every echo of praise that falls from
your lips.

He draws near to you and brings you
comfort and a chance to feel His presence.
You can then thank Him for everything you
are and have.

An attitude of praise is an attitude of
prayer. Surrender to it, release the day's
concerns, the circumstances that are out of
your control and the weariness of your heart,
and let God meet you in the praise circle.

"Whoever offers praise glorifies Me;
and to him who orders his conduct aright
I will show the salvation of God."

PSALM 50:23 NKJV

From the rising of the sun to its going down,
the LORD's name is to be praised.
PSALM 113:3 NKJV

♡♡♡♡

"The master was full of praise. 'Well done,
my good and faithful servant. You have
been faithful in handling this small
amount, so now I will give you many more
responsibilities. Let's celebrate together!'"
MATTHEW 25:21 NLT

♡♡♡♡

Then they believed His words;
they sang His praise.
PSALM 106:12 NASB

Let every created thing give praise to
the LORD, for he issued his command,
and they came into being. He set
them in place forever and ever.
PSALM 148:5–6 NLT

♡♡♡♡

Let everything that has breath
praise the LORD. Praise the LORD.
PSALM 150:6 NIV

♡♡♡♡

The crucible is for silver and the
furnace for gold, and each is tested
by the praise accorded him.
PROVERBS 27:21 NASB

It is good to proclaim your unfailing
love in the morning, your faithfulness
in the evening, accompanied by
the ten-string instrument, a harp,
and the melody of a lyre.

PSALM 92:2–3 NLT

By Him let us continually offer the sacrifice
of praise to God, that is, the fruit of our
lips, giving thanks to His name.

HEBREWS 13:15 NKJV

Let heaven and earth praise him,
the seas and all that move in them.

PSALM 69:34 NIV

Praying

If you align your heart's intentions with God, you're more likely to do the thing you mean to do. Prayer gives you the opportunity to invite God into your situation. It helps you take the time to think twice about what you'll do. It gives God a chance to create a bigger space in your heart to receive the blessings He has for you.

Make prayer part of your heart's intentions every day. You'll find that more of your plans will succeed because you'll take the actions you mean to take. You won't be disappointed by what you do because you'll succeed at doing the right thing.

I love the LORD because he hears
my voice and my prayer for mercy.
Because he bends down to listen,
I will pray as long as I have breath!
PSALM 116:1–2 NLT

He saw that there was no man,
and wondered that there was no
intercessor; therefore His own arm
brought salvation for Him; and His
own righteousness, it sustained Him.

Isaiah 59:16 nkjv

♡♡♡♡

Now when Daniel knew that the document
was signed, he entered his house (now
in his roof chamber he had windows open
toward Jerusalem); and he continued
kneeling on his knees three times a day,
praying and giving thanks before his God,
as he had been doing previously.

Daniel 6:10 nasb

♡♡♡♡

Be anxious for nothing, but in everything by
prayer and supplication, with thanksgiving,
let your requests be made known to God.

Philippians 4:6 nkjv

We also pray that you will be strengthened with all his glorious power so you will have all the endurance and patience you need.

COLOSSIANS 1:11 NLT

♡♡♡♡

"O my God, incline Your ear and hear! Open Your eyes and see our desolations and the city which is called by Your name; for we are not presenting our supplications before You on account of any merits of our own, but on account of Your great compassion."

DANIEL 9:18 NASB

♡♡♡♡

Since we could not get Paul to change his mind, we gave up and prayed, "Lord, please make us willing to do what you want."

ACTS 21:14 CEV

And pray in the Spirit on all occasions
with all kinds of prayers and requests.
With this in mind, be alert and always
keep on praying for all the Lord's people.
EPHESIANS 6:18 NIV

Devote yourselves to prayer,
being watchful and thankful.
COLOSSIANS 4:2 NIV

Never stop praying.
1 THESSALONIANS 5:17 NLT

Priorities

You've probably been saying the Lord's Prayer for years. You say it, you believe it, and you end it with, "Thy will be done."

When you question whether you're doing God's will or your own, put everything else aside and ask God directly. Make it a priority to find out. God will lead you as long as you're truly interested in where He wants you to go. You must seek His will with your whole heart, and if your heart is not ready, you must be willing for Him to shape it even more. Sometimes we need God's help to change our minds and live more heart-shaped lives.

"You will seek the LORD your God, and you will find Him if you search for Him with all your heart and all your soul."
DEUTERONOMY 4:29 NASB

As long as he sought the LORD,
God gave him success.

2 CHRONICLES 26:5 NIV

♡♡♡♡

You, God, are my God, earnestly I seek
you; I thirst for you, my whole being
longs for you, in a dry and parched
land where there is no water.

PSALM 63:1 NIV

♡♡♡♡

May my tongue cling to the roof of my
mouth if I do not remember you, if I do
not exalt Jerusalem above my chief joy.

PSALM 137:6 NASB

"Seek first the kingdom of God and
His righteousness, and all these
things shall be added to you."
MATTHEW 6:33 NKJV

♡ ♡ ♡ ♡

John bore witness of Him and cried out,
saying, "This was He of whom I said,
'He who comes after me is preferred
before me, for He was before me.'"
JOHN 1:15 NKJV

♡ ♡ ♡ ♡

And they exceeded our expectations:
They gave themselves first of all to the Lord,
and then by the will of God also to us.
2 CORINTHIANS 8:5 NIV

Our people must learn to do good by meeting the urgent needs of others; then they will not be unproductive.

Titus 3:14 NLT

♡♡♡♡

Dear children, keep away from anything that might take God's place in your hearts.

1 John 5:21 NLT

♡♡♡♡

And they entered into a covenant to seek the LORD God of their fathers with all their heart and with all their soul.

2 Chronicles 15:12 KJV

Purpose

You may be wondering what your purpose is or whether you can make any real difference in the world. You do have a purpose, and no one but you can accomplish the work you are meant to do. You're on a mission.

God works through you and shapes your heart to carry out His purposes with love and mercy. He knows every detail and wants you to draw near to Him for strength and wisdom. His intention is for you to succeed in every good way. Work with Him and fulfill your purpose in Him.

The LORD will accomplish what concerns me;
Your lovingkindness, O LORD, is everlasting;
do not forsake the works of Your hands.

PSALM 138:8 NASB

Commit to the LORD whatever you do,
and he will establish your plans.

PROVERBS 16:3 NIV

♡♡♡♡

So, my dear brothers and sisters, be strong
and immovable. Always work enthusiastically
for the Lord, for you know that nothing you
do for the Lord is ever useless.

1 CORINTHIANS 15:58 NLT

♡♡♡♡

"I know that You can do all things, and that
no purpose of Yours can be thwarted."

JOB 42:2 NASB

Every way of a man is right in his own
eyes, but the LORD weighs the hearts.

PROVERBS 21:2 NKJV

♡♡♡♡

"For I know the plans I have for you,"
says the LORD. "They are plans for
good and not for disaster, to give
you a future and a hope."

JEREMIAH 29:11 NLT

♡♡♡♡

"I have come down from heaven,
not to do My own will, but the
will of Him who sent Me."

JOHN 6:38 NASB

For we are His workmanship, created
in Christ Jesus for good works,
which God prepared beforehand
so that we would walk in them.

EPHESIANS 2:10 NASB

For everything, absolutely everything,
above and below, visible and invisible. . .
everything got started in him and
finds its purpose in him.

COLOSSIANS 1:16 MSG

I delight to do thy will, O my God:
yea, thy law is within my heart.

PSALM 40:8 KJV

Restoration

It is said God can do wonders with a broken heart if we are willing to give Him all the pieces. Your heart is a matter of deep concern to God, and He seeks to protect it in any way possible. He does it best when you remain close to Him.

If your heart is broken by insults or rejection, go back to the Source of your strength—your Father—and put your hand in His. Tell Him all you feel; give Him all the pieces so He can help you mend again.

When you do, you will be restored. Thank God that He always mends a broken heart.

"If My people who are called by My name will humble themselves, and pray and seek My face, and turn from their wicked ways, then I will hear from heaven, and will forgive their sin and heal their land."

2 Chronicles 7:14 nkjv

Restore to me the joy of your salvation and grant me a willing spirit, to sustain me.

PSALM 51:12 NIV

♡♡♡♡

"Then your salvation will come like the dawn, and your wounds will quickly heal. Your godliness will lead you forward, and the glory of the LORD will protect you from behind."

ISAIAH 58:8 NLT

♡♡♡♡

"I will give them hearts that recognize me as the LORD. They will be my people, and I will be their God, for they will return to me wholeheartedly."

JEREMIAH 24:7 NLT

Then the Angel showed me Water-of-Life River, crystal bright. It flowed from the Throne of God and the Lamb, right down the middle of the street. The Tree of Life was planted on each side of the River, producing twelve kinds of fruit, a ripe fruit each month. The leaves of the Tree are for healing the nations.

REVELATION 22:1–2 MSG

"Return, faithless people;
I will cure you of backsliding."

JEREMIAH 3:22 NIV

He said to the man, "Stretch out your hand." And he stretched it out, and his hand was restored.

MARK 3:5 NASB

He will again have compassion on us; He will tread our iniquities under foot. Yes, You will cast all their sins into the depths of the sea.

MICAH 7:19 NASB

And the prayer offered in faith will restore the one who is sick, and the Lord will raise him up, and if he has committed sins, they will be forgiven him.

JAMES 5:15 NASB

He restores my soul.

PSALM 23:3 NASB

Righteousness

We like to think we know right from wrong, good from evil, and love from hate. But many people appear to live according to what they believe is right in their own eyes.

Living according to the "gospel of you" breaks down if you believe it's okay to steal a car from a driveway, kidnap a child, or steal someone's identity.

How can you live with Jesus in your heart? You can seek Him and try to please Him in ways that are right in His eyes. If you wonder whether something you may do is right or wrong, ask the One who still reigns. . . yesterday, today and forever.

Noah was a righteous man, blameless among the people of his time, and he walked faithfully with God.
GENESIS 6:9 NIV

So David reigned over all Israel;
and David administered justice and
righteousness for all his people.

2 SAMUEL 8:15 NASB

♡♡♡♡

The LORD knows the way of the righteous,
but the way of the ungodly shall perish.

PSALM 1:6 NKJV

♡♡♡♡

I will greatly rejoice in the LORD, my soul
shall be joyful in my God; for He has clothed
me with the garments of salvation, He has
covered me with the robe of righteousness.

ISAIAH 61:10 NKJV

[The LORD] is my rock, and there
is no unrighteousness in Him.

PSALM 92:15 NASB

♡♡♡♡

"I said, 'Plant the good seeds of
righteousness, and you will harvest a crop
of love. Plow up the hard ground of
your hearts, for now is the time to seek
the LORD, that he may come and
shower righteousness upon you.'"

HOSEA 10:12 NLT

♡♡♡♡

The righteous will live by his faith.

HABAKKUK 2:4 NASB

Stand your ground, putting on the
belt of truth and the body armor
of God's righteousness.

EPHESIANS 6:14 NLT

Not having my own righteousness,
which is from the law, but that which is
through faith in Christ, the righteousness
which is from God by faith.

PHILIPPIANS 3:9 NKJV

[Abram] believed in the LORD, and He
accounted it to him for righteousness.

GENESIS 15:6 NKJV

Self-Control

Warriors of old, or even warriors today, may not agree that having self-control is better than conquering a city. But conquering a city took a lot of soldiers and strength.

Perhaps conquering the self is more similar than we think. Perhaps overcoming our own weaknesses takes more discipline, exercise, and shaping up to maintain self-control than we've considered.

If patience is power, then self-control is what conquers the city of our discontent and offers us true strength. Look at the temptations around you that may inspire self-control. Let God help you maintain the kind of control that will benefit your life in the best ways.

People with understanding control their anger; a hot temper shows great foolishness.
PROVERBS 14:29 NLT

Control yourselves and be careful!
The devil, your enemy, goes around
like a roaring lion looking for someone
to eat. Refuse to give in to him, by
standing strong in your faith.

1 Peter 5:8–9 ncv

♡♡♡♡

The fruit of the Spirit is. . .self-control.

Galatians 5:22–23 nasb

♡♡♡♡

A wise man restrains his anger and
overlooks insults. This is to his credit.

Proverbs 19:11 tlb

Everyone who competes in the games
exercises self-control in all things.

1 CORINTHIANS 9:25 NASB

Everyone must be quick to hear,
slow to speak and slow to anger;
for the anger of man does not
achieve the righteousness of God.

JAMES 1:19–20 NASB

We belong to the day,
so we should control ourselves.

1 THESSALONIANS 5:8 NCV

He must be. . .self-controlled,
upright, holy and disciplined.
TITUS 1:7–8 NIV

So prepare your minds for action
and exercise self-control.
1 PETER 1:13 NLT

Controlling your temper is
better than capturing a city.
PROVERBS 16:32 NCV

Selflessness

Have you ever felt slightly depressed and, before you know it, found yourself curled up in a little ball? Everything is suddenly about you and what is or isn't happening to you.

When you feel like that, let go of thinking about yourself and start to think about others.

If you step out of your world for a few minutes and reach out to help someone else, you might discover things look different and you're not alone. Lending a helping hand takes your focus off your own troubles and helps you feel better. Helping others is a sure cure for what ails you.

But Daniel purposed in his heart that he would not defile himself with the portion of the king's delicacies, nor with the wine which he drank; therefore he requested of the chief of the eunuchs that he might not defile himself.

DANIEL 1:8 NKJV

She looks well to the ways of her household,
and does not eat the bread of idleness.

PROVERBS 31:27 NASB

Then Jesus said to His disciples,
"If anyone desires to come after Me,
let him deny himself and take up his
cross and follow Me. For whoever desires
to save his life will lose it, but whoever
loses his life for My sake will find it."

MATTHEW 16:24–25 NKJV

"I am the good shepherd. The good shepherd sacrifices his life for the sheep."

JOHN 10:11 NLT

"As the Father knows Me, even so I know the Father, and I lay down My life for the sheep. . . . Therefore My Father loves Me, because I lay down My life that I may take it again. No one takes it from Me, but I lay it down of Myself."

JOHN 10:15, 17–18 NKJV

♡♡♡♡

No one should seek their own good, but the good of others.

1 CORINTHIANS 10:24 NIV

♡♡♡♡

Love does not parade itself, is not puffed up; does not behave rudely, does not seek its own.

1 CORINTHIANS 13:4–5 NKJV

Share each other's burdens, and in this way obey the law of Christ. If you think you are too important to help someone, you are only fooling yourself. You are not that important.

GALATIANS 6:2–3 NLT

♡♡♡♡

Let each of you look out not only for his own interests, but also for the interests of others.

PHILIPPIANS 2:4 NKJV

♡♡♡♡

And this world is fading away, along with everything that people crave. But anyone who does what pleases God will live forever.

1 JOHN 2:17 NLT

Serving

When Jesus commanded us to love God with our whole heart, He meant we should do so with every breath, every opportunity, every service we might render. He meant we should be committed to living with all the energy, gusto, and goodness we could muster.

We live wholeheartedly because we want to honor Him. Look at the things you're doing today. See if you can discover the moments you're serving God with great energy and enthusiasm, rather than simply doing a mindless task with no purpose or joy.

Awaken your spirit to the gift of serving with a heart of joy. It'll make your whole day go better.

"So fear the LORD and serve
him wholeheartedly."
JOSHUA 24:14 NLT

"If we are thrown into the blazing furnace, the God whom we serve is able to save us. He will rescue us from your power, Your Majesty."

DANIEL 3:17 NLT

♡♡♡♡

"Whoever wishes to become great among you shall be your servant, and whoever wishes to be first among you shall be your slave; just as the Son of Man did not come to be served, but to serve, and to give His life a ransom for many."

MATTHEW 20:26–28 NASB

♡♡♡♡

"Love your enemies. Let them bring out the best in you, not the worst. When someone gives you a hard time, respond with the energies of prayer for that person. If someone slaps you in the face, stand there and take it. If someone grabs your shirt, giftwrap your best coat and make a present of it. If someone takes unfair advantage of you, use the occasion to practice the servant life."

LUKE 6:27–30 MSG

But Martha was distracted with all her preparations; and she came up to Him and said, "Lord, do You not care that my sister has left me to do all the serving alone? Then tell her to help me." But the Lord answered and said to her, "Martha, Martha, you are worried and bothered about so many things; but only one thing is necessary, for Mary has chosen the good part, which shall not be taken away from her."

LUKE 10:40–42 NASB

♡♡♡♡

Those who have believing masters, let them not despise them because they are brethren, but rather serve them because those who are benefited are believers and beloved.

1 TIMOTHY 6:2 NKJV

♡♡♡♡

Serve wholeheartedly, as if you were serving the Lord, not people, because you know that the Lord will reward each one for whatever good they do.

EPHESIANS 6:7–8 NIV

Through love serve one another.
GALATIANS 5:13 NASB

♥♥♥♥

Make sure you don't take things for
granted and go slack in working for the
common good; share what you have with
others. God takes particular pleasure
in acts of worship—a different kind of
"sacrifice"—that take place in kitchen
and workplace and on the streets.
HEBREWS 13:16 MSG

♥♥♥♥

Do your work willingly, as though
you were serving the Lord himself.
COLOSSIANS 3:23 CEV

Speech

We've all experienced the angry words of another person, whether justified or not. In receiving those same words, we've had to choose how to respond. Should we come back with more anger and harsh words? Or should we respond gently, offering the olive branch of peace?

What we say is so important to the well-being of others and to the spirit within each of us that we must be very conscious of our words, our tone, and our intentions any time we speak. We must remember to protect the hearts of others in our interactions. Let our words always be shared for the good of another.

Let the words of my mouth, and the
meditation of my heart, be acceptable
in thy sight, O LORD, my strength,
and my redeemer.
PSALM 19:14 KJV

Keep your tongue from evil and
your lips from speaking deceit.

PSALM 34:13 NASB

♡♡♡♡

Beautiful words stir my heart. I will recite
a lovely poem about the king, for my
tongue is like the pen of a skillful poet.

PSALM 45:1 NLT

♡♡♡♡

A word fitly spoken is like apples of gold
in settings of silver. Like an earring of
gold and an ornament of fine gold is a
wise rebuker to an obedient ear.

PROVERBS 25:11–12 NKJV

"By your words you will be justified, and by
your words you will be condemned."
MATTHEW 12:37 ESV

Speaking the truth in love. . .
EPHESIANS 4:15 NASB

Let no unwholesome word proceed
from your mouth, but only such a word
as is good for edification according
to the need of the moment, so that it
will give grace to those who hear.
EPHESIANS 4:29 NASB

Be filled with the Spirit. Speak to each
other with psalms, hymns, and spiritual
songs, singing, and making music
in your hearts to the Lord.

EPHESIANS 5:18–19 NCV

Let your speech always be with grace,
seasoned with salt, that you may know
how you ought to answer each one.

COLOSSIANS 4:6 NKJV

The tongue of the wise brings healing.

PROVERBS 12:18 NASB

Trust

Worry is one of those heart matters that often reflects your faith. If you believe God is taking care of you, then you know the basics are covered and you trust things are going okay. But you give in to worry just the same.

God is always caring for you, and all you have to do is believe He is. Nothing will come into your life that will surprise Him, and He will do all He can to help you with everything. Raise your faith, not your doubts. Sweep out the worries and relax in God's care. Give your heart a rest today and let worry bother someone else.

"Put your trust in the LORD your God and you will be established."
2 CHRONICLES 20:20 NASB

Trust in the LORD with all your heart;
do not depend on your own understanding.
Seek his will in all you do, and he will
show you which path to take.

PROVERBS 3:5–6 NLT

♥♥♥♥

I trust in God's unfailing
love forever and ever.

PSALM 52:8 NIV

♥♥♥♥

When I am afraid, I will put my trust in
You. In God, whose word I praise, in God
I have put my trust; I shall not be afraid.
What can mere man do to me?

PSALM 56:3–4 NASB

Trust in Him at all times, you people;
pour out your heart before Him;
God is a refuge for us.

PSALM 62:8 NKJV

♡♡♡♡

I will say to the LORD, "My refuge and
my fortress, my God, in whom I trust."

PSALM 91:2 ESV

♡♡♡♡

It is better to take refuge in the LORD than
to trust in man. It is better to take refuge
in the LORD than to trust in princes.

PSALM 118:8-9 NASB

But those who trust in the LORD will find new strength. They will soar high on wings like eagles. They will run and not grow weary. They will walk and not faint.

ISAIAH 40:31 NLT

♡♡♡♡

Give all your worries and cares to God, for he cares about you.

1 PETER 5:7 NLT

♡♡♡♡

Many are the woes of the wicked, but the LORD's unfailing love surrounds the one who trusts in him.

PSALM 32:10 NIV

Wisdom

What is wisdom? We may think the wisest people today are Rhodes scholars or great scientists or inventors. We often equate wisdom with intellect or being smart. We strive to be smarter than someone else so we can stay slightly ahead of them. Does that mean we're wise?

The "wisdom of heaven" appears to be different, though. It is about being considerate and showing mercy or kindness. It's about being peaceful and leading with a heart shaped by love. This kind of wisdom, the kind that brings inner peace, is the one for which we pray.

May your loving heart guide you into true wisdom in all of your relationships.

"And he said to man, 'Behold, the fear of the Lord, that is wisdom, and to turn away from evil is understanding.'"
JOB 28:28 ESV

My child, listen to what I say, and treasure
my commands. Tune your ears to wisdom,
and concentrate on understanding. Cry
out for insight, and ask for understanding.
Search for them as you would for silver;
seek them like hidden treasures.

PROVERBS 2:1–4 NLT

♡♡♡♡

The fear of the LORD is the beginning
of wisdom, and the knowledge of
the Holy One is understanding.

PROVERBS 9:10 NASB

♡♡♡♡

God made the earth by his power. He used
his wisdom to build the world and his
understanding to stretch out the skies.

JEREMIAH 10:12 NCV

Oh the depth of the riches both of the wisdom and knowledge of God! How unsearchable are His judgments and His ways past finding out!

ROMANS 11:33 NKJV

♡♡♡♡

From childhood you have been acquainted with the sacred writings, which are able to make you wise for salvation through faith in Christ Jesus.

2 TIMOTHY 3:15 ESV

♡♡♡♡

If any of you lacks wisdom, let him ask of God, who gives to all generously and without reproach, and it will be given to him. But he must ask in faith without any doubting, for the one who doubts is like the surf of the sea, driven and tossed by the wind.

JAMES 1:5-6 NASB

Let the word of Christ dwell
in you richly in all wisdom.
COLOSSIANS 3:16 NKJV

Real wisdom, God's wisdom, begins
with a holy life and is characterized by
getting along with others. It is gentle
and reasonable, overflowing with mercy
and blessings, not hot one day and cold
the next, not two-faced. You can develop
a healthy, robust community that lives
right with God and enjoy its results only
if you do the hard work of getting along
with each other, treating each other
with dignity and honor.
JAMES 3:17–18 MSG

Teach us to use wisely
all the time we have.
PSALM 90:12 CEV

Witness

We talk a lot about witnessing to our faith.
Some of us do it with great gusto, wearing
our faith on our clothing, dropping it into our
text messages, practically flaunting it.

Some of us share our hearts in quieter
ways—by lending a hand when needed, en-
couraging those around us with our positive
spirits and generous hearts, praying faithfully
for people, and adding one more potato to
the pot when someone comes by unexpect-
edly at dinner time. All of those things help
us to be steadfast defenders of our faith.
They serve as an example of our love for the
Lord.

> "I will also make you a light for the
> Gentiles, that my salvation may
> reach to the ends of the earth."
> ISAIAH 49:6 NIV

Those who have insight will shine
brightly like the brightness of the
expanse of heaven, and those who
lead the many to righteousness,
like the stars forever and ever.

DANIEL 12:3 NASB

♡♡♡♡

"Go therefore and make disciples of all
nations, baptizing them in the name of the
Father and of the Son and of the Holy Spirit,
teaching them to observe all that I have
commanded you. And behold, I am with
you always, to the end of the age."

MATTHEW 28:19–20 ESV

♡♡♡♡

There was a man sent from God whose
name was John. He came as a witness
to testify concerning that light, so that
through him all might believe.

JOHN 1:6–7 NIV

John testified saying, "I have seen the Spirit descending as a dove out of heaven, and He remained upon Him. I did not recognize Him, but He who sent me to baptize in water said to me, 'He upon whom you see the Spirit descending and remaining upon Him, this is the One who baptizes in the Holy Spirit.' I myself have seen, and have testified that this is the Son of God."

JOHN 1:32–34 NASB

♡♡♡♡

"But you will receive power when the Holy Spirit comes on you; and you will be my witnesses in Jerusalem, and in all Judea and Samaria, and to the ends of the earth."

ACTS 1:8 NIV

♡♡♡♡

Preach the word; be ready in season and out of season; reprove, rebuke, and exhort, with complete patience and teaching.

2 TIMOTHY 4:2 ESV

Therefore, since we have so great a cloud of witnesses surrounding us, let us also lay aside every encumbrance and the sin which so easily entangles us, and let us run with endurance the race that is set before us.

HEBREWS 12:1 NASB

But sanctify the Lord God in your hearts, and always be ready to give a defense to everyone who asks you a reason for the hope that is in you, with meekness and fear; having a good conscience, that when they defame you as evildoers, those who revile your good conduct in Christ may be ashamed.

1 PETER 3:15–16 NKJV

"You are the light of the world."

MATTHEW 5:14 NKJV

Check Out More of the
Heart-Shaped Series!

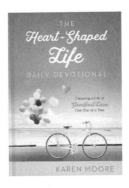

The Heart-Shaped Life Daily Devotional

Readers will be motivated to live a heart-shaped life with this inspiring daily devotional from Barbour Publishing. With refreshing thoughts, prayers, and scripture selections, *The Heart-Shaped Life Daily Devotional* will help readers discover the best path to the good life. . .which is LOVE.

Hardback / 978-1-68322-009-1 / $14.99